the words

i never said

-chloe hopper

these words

are my salvation,

my secret,

my hope,

i have never spoke them before,

and they have helped me to heal.

this is the recipe

to a happy

healthy life,

these words heal,

and protect

let these words teach you

about

the mind

the heart

reality

acceptance

and hope

contents

mind

12

anxiety is silent,

a quiet voice

coming from the dark

and becoming the loudest voice in the room

depression formed a life in black and white

while everyone else's was in colour

how rare

and beautiful it is

to exist at the same time as you

how to heal your mood

1) cry, let it all out

2) breathe

3) learn how to say no

4) understand there is always a light

5) find where your love lies

6) decide if the dark is worth it

7) dance to your favourite music

8) write it all down

9) know you will be okay

i am in the darkest point in my life,

please show me the light

i'll start to be gentle

when i can live

and the voice

stays silent

i'm terrified of living,

i'm scared of so much,

what if i don't meet their expectations,

what if i don't find someone and i grow up

alone,

what if i have nothing,

what if i don't tell them i love them,

what if i keep on hurting

and failing

and breaking

i envy the person

who now receives your love

i feel disconnected from my body

-separate

i feel i should apologise

to the young me

whose being i would spend

each night

picking apart

i feel the urge to survive

and stop surviving

at the same time

-confusion

i find i either

overthink the past

or worry about the future,

so much that i am never

living in the now

i live with my body and my mind

but we all seem so distant

-disconnected

it feels like i'm watching my life through a fuzzy pair of old glasses, i feel distanced from the people around me, a separate entity. i feel like a passenger in my own body, foreign and unknown. i am a shell of the person i used to be, like a piece in a game of chess, being moved and controlled. when i close my eyes i fall into a void of nothingness and i forget what feeling feels like. my heart drops to the floor when my brain remembers i am alive and have to face the day. i want to be able to touch things and them feel real. i want the normality and stability in my life back, please.

my body

has etched my life into my body

in countless scars

like the constellations in the sky

like fate deciding my path

in life for me

my mind has started to embrace the dark

corners

in which it finds reasons

why i am not worthy of your love

the day you left me

my heart snapped inside of my body

the depression didn't shatter my heart

and the anxiety didn't lessen my soul,

i am still the same girl,

just with more torture

the worst part about all of this is that

as i rip my heart into pieces

and my cheeks are covered in salty rivers,

you don't even pay me a single thought

this is my therapy session

why did you hurt me?

i thought we were forever

why didn't i leave

when he made my world so small

and slowly chipped away at my heart

why do i keep letting my mind

convince me i am worthless

why is it

that the things we long for the most

are always the furthest

from our reach

don't pay attention

to what the inner voice

is saying

he told me

you look tired

i'm exhausted

i tell him,

i've been fighting my own head for years

now

what else do you expect?

i measure my self worth

based on how many people love me

but no matter

how many do,

it will never be enough

i prayed each night

to whichever god would listen

that my pain may leave

and stop tearing my heart,

at least my work

kept me busy

and distracted

that the hurt never fully consumed me,

i guess i should be grateful

but i still feel hate towards the force that

made me hurt so much,

no matter how much i tried to relax

my mind was swimming deep in another

universe

i thought i could

accomplish being happy

by tricking my brain,

i didn't know it would

just make me more numb

i used to cry myself to sleep

because i couldn't find a man

to complete me,

now i cry because he has chipped more from

my soul

than being alone ever did

i want you to break me,

hammer into me

and shatter my heart,

i just want you to make me feel again,

please

-i'm tired of being empty

what do i do with someone

who only wants to change me

i don't know when it started,

when my mind started giving me more pain

than love,

maybe i was born with it

maybe it joined me

that one night

when i thought hurting myself would solve

all my problems

or maybe when i stepped foot in that new

school

and was surrounded by strangers

i don't know,

maybe it was nothing and i was born with a

heart destined to give me more pain than

kindness,

or maybe it was everything at once

45

to live in happiness,

you have to accept

those uncomfortable feelings

my pain

is the reason

i started writing poetry,

to turn my scars

into words

and heal my broken heart

scream

shout

yell at the world,

curse them

for creating your life

with so much torture,

let it all out

-release

wake up, get dressed, eat, go to school.

learn, remember, write.

come home, revise, eat, revise, cry, sleep.

wake up the next day to do the same thing

over and over again.

that's school life,

being taught how to multiply,

trigonometry or how to analyse a poem.

instead of being taught something that will

actually help us.

school is supposed to be safe,

but we go there with a full heart and leave

each day with it more shattered than the last.

they tell us that 'this is the way to a full life'

but i can't remember the last time i truly

lived,

the last time i truly enjoyed myself.

i wish i could go to school and laugh with

my friends, wear what makes me

comfortable and not have to think about

being written up for 'inappropriate clothing'

i want to be myself but school makes me be

somebody else.

why do you say you're teaching us for reality

when you teach us nothing about how to

look after ourselves or how to be ourselves

-is this supposed to be fair?

heart

a mother's love

is more powerful

than any romantic love

as you trace your finger

gently across my back

i am falling in love all over again

can we be lovers forever?

please

even if they took away

all that we had

we could still conjure up

our love,

as it comes from the bones in our aching

bodies

and the depths of our soul,

it comes from us

i can only fall asleep

when your body

is cradling mine,

only then can my body

and mind

relax

i'm not afraid of love,

i'm just afraid of losing you

i kept trying to leave

but my lungs heaved,

gasping for the air i breathe

when i'm with you

i longed to bring back

that last bouquet of flowers

you bought me

as they are now wilting in their vase

falling off

one

by

one,

they were all i had left of you

i miss the days with my friends

when we knew every detail about each other,

and would skip up and down the playground

arms linked tightly

talking about what we'd do at our sleepover

that night,

when we would talk and talk, too lost to even

register time,

when we would play dress up and take

ourselves to a magical world,

when we would win and celebrate with

cheers and chocolate cake,

when we danced in the rain

and jumped in the puddles,

being older has starved me of this fun,

this freedom,

i miss being a kid

-nostalgia

i need you to ignore everything you may

think you know about love and think of one

thing only,

respect

respect them with all you have,

give it to them and they will give it to you,

be equal in your love

and it will thrive

i spend each single night

away from you

wishing to bring you back to me

i think i have found my person

in you

i think i lost my sadness

and pain

the day i laid my eyes on you

i think i would give my soul

to be yours

i tried my best

to delete the memories of you

from my mind

but my heart

holds onto you too strongly

that i can't

let them go

i want someone to look at me

in my eyes

and just know that i am the one,

i want them to tell their friends about me,

how their heart beats faster when i walk into

the room

and tell their mum their plans with me in the

future,

i just want to belong to someone

it took loving myself

to realise i shouldn't

be afraid of love

look me in the eyes

when you're breaking my heart,

if you don't

then at least i know you're human

my body is burning

from the heat of wanting you,

i want our love

to transcend

time and space,

i want eye contact

and touches like electricity,

i want this to change us

my years with you

make me think the best years of my life

have been

and the future

won't be as good

nothing can compare

to how she makes me feel

staying when it only hurts

is not love

when i tell you

i love you,

it also means

you're the only one for me,

i don't know how to leave you,

i don't want to live a life without you,

i hope you know that

i can't live without you

yesterday

another pair of hands

caressed your body

and i punished them for doing what i once

did

-jealousy

you can't offer people your broken heart

you hurt me

and then tell me you love me,

stop playing with my heart

you kept leaving

but i kept craving your company

you showed me love

and i am eternally grateful

your fingers touch my cheek

as they come back with a singular eyelash

make a wish

you said

so i close my eyes

but cannot make a wish

for all that i want

is already here with me

your lips caress my scars

and you tell me

you're safe with me my love

and I think

i have found my home

nothing tastes sweeter

than loving yourself

on days i could not move

and the earth seemed too dark to face,

you came and washed my face

and nursed me back to life,

thank you

reality

i'm not a victim of my life,

but a warrior

of what you put me through

i don't want to live in a world

which thinks that

women are still objects

under a man's thumb

i've never seen a mountain and wished that it
were smaller

or swam in an ocean and questioned why it
was so deep,

or walked through a forest and asked why it
has so many leaves,

so why do you question your being?

why do you ask someone in the sky why you
were born?

you were created of stardust and space,

you deserve to survive,

no, you deserve to live

it offered my heart

such relief

when i realised

the pain that it faces

is felt by so many

remember the difference between feeling

down

and completely shattered

a partner can't complete you in the ways you

need completing,

only you can do that

don't preach for feminism if it doesn't

include

trans,

black,

asian,

or gay

women

for a world that doesn't want my body

to belong to myself,

it focuses a lot

on my pleasure

i am not disposable

i'm tired of the energy it's taking

for me to hate myself

-why do i do it?

i'm finding it difficult to see

the difference between

violence

and love

-they look the same

you can love yourself,

but don't flaunt it.

have your own opinions,

but don't show them off.

love who you want,

as long as its not the same gender.

be smart,

but not cocky.

-welcome to society

i have a very unhealthy relationship

with the body i was born in,

it gives me life

and does nothing but care for me

but i show it nothing but cruelty and

disrespect,

why is this?

i kept trying

to fit into a society

that never wanted me

i won't pretend to be less

intelligent,

comfortable,

or beautiful

to please a man,

to make him feel better for his lack of them

if you don't love yourself

you'll have nothing

isn't it sad

us women can't live safely

with society's rapists

in our lives,

imagine what we could accomplish

without them

no amount of external work

will fill the internal hole

begging for attention

remember to tell yourself

that what they did to you,

and your bad days,

and what happened

doesn't make you a bad person,

they're not you

i really don't understand why society is so
cruel,

why do they preach to love ourselves

but then put us into boxes based on a number

on a scale,

a number which determines your worth,

why are we never enough for them?

it's either too thin or too fat,

too tall or too short,

what do we have to do to get them to accept

us?

the earth takes care of you,

don't betray it

why are we taught

that straight

is the default

why didn't i leave you sooner?

-revelations

you can't give me anything

i can't give myself

-reality check

you can't create art

if you don't live

-art comes with life

you can't silence someone

who was brought up

with tape on their mouth

you didn't lose your happiness,

it was just hiding from you

your soul won't become complete

by what you achieve

or how you look

or how much you eat,

no matter what you do

you'll always be searching for that one thing

to fill that hole in your heart,

your soul only aches for

love and connection

if you hadn't been forced into it,

you never would have started

-perspective

no one

regrets recovering

from what almost killed them

no one in this world

is blinder

than the white straight cis male

who despite everything

still doesn't believe

in racism and sexism

and all the world's tortures

what do you have to gain

by filling your mind

with self doubt

start to reject their ideas

of what the perfect woman

should look like

why does it affect

the white man so much

what a woman does with her body,

he wouldn't survive a day in her shoes

you grow stronger

from every heartbreak

you told me i was too opinionated

like it was an insult,

the thing is

i have too many views

for your small brain to comprehend

acceptance

i have a fear

that i'm not living up to what people want of

me,

see i have no hope for my life

but worry constantly about not succeeding,

high functioning depression

they call it

i worry i am wasting my time,

not working hard enough

or fast enough

or not doing enough work,

i tell my mum,

i'll eat at school

because i am scared what they'll think of me

if the jeans i just bought

become too small,

if i sit down to breakfast in the morning

then i have to talk to them

and if i talk to them they'll realise how

my brain works

if i don't focus on my school work

i'll fail

and then my mind will show me more pain

than my body can handle,

but what's the point in focusing too hard,

because it's not worth it,

right?

i only put my energy into things

that will bring me closer to my dreams,

but i learnt not to dream too big

from my mother

who told me

anything you don't love,

isn't worth it

i put every hour in my day into

working

studying

writing

doing anything to improve myself

in hopes they won't leave,

because why wouldn't they?

i have a hope for the future,

but voices telling me they're useless

-what do i do?

accept that perfection is impossible,

stop obsessing over what you can't change

i'm beginning to realise

i'll never fully be complete in someone

else's company

for it is only my own love

to myself

that will complete me

i'm learning i have to respect

my mind

body

and soul

to survive this journey

i found my confidence

when i learnt how to be happy

in my own skin

and when i realised

having fun

is more important

than how you look to others

-perspective is key

it took me two years

to realise

you can't make someone love you

our world is busy

and is filled with so many people

that it's hard to remember

that the only opinion that matters

is your own,

you don't need to chase validation

from anyone

except yourself,

and life will continue on through the noise

if their opinion

differs from your own

self love

isn't

loving the nice things about yourself

yet it is

accepting the parts of ourselves

that are difficult

and tough

and cruel

there's nothing wrong with you

i promise,

you're growing,

transforming,

saving yourself,

it'll be okay

you already have

the things that will complete you

you will only have this version of yourself

once

-cherish the now

your opinion of yourself

is the only one that matters

you can't offer people

a heart

that is already broken

your voice

will lead you

to freedom

i'm truly starting to like myself,

not love, i don't think i'm there yet,

but definitely like.

i like the way my hair falls around my face

and how my face looks when it catches the

light.

i'm beginning to like waking up in the

morning to see the person looking back at

me, seeing her smile and laugh and sing to

herself.

the way i talk to others and put my energy

into bettering myself, how i write poetry and

paint and express myself.

i'm starting to realise that it's ok to like

yourself

i'm done

trying to prove myself

to the people

that don't matter

don't put your energy into people

who don't give you theirs

us humans believe

that when we are lost

we can find ourselves again

by getting onto our knees

and praying to some god

that our soul is brought back to us,

we think improving ourselves

will speed up the process

and help us get to ourselves again

but in reality

you'll never truly find yourself,

you constantly grow

and change

every day

and every month,

your self which is full

149

and true

is you now,

today,

right in this moment,

instead of trying to find yourself,

find the thing to help you live

in the wonderful strong life

you live now

-you are already complete

i was always taught to work harder than

everyone else in the room

as that is what will make me valuable and

important

you are not alone,

i promise

you belong exactly where you are

-home

you have only scratched the surface

of all the things

you are capable of

eight things you should know about me

one. i have a really big heart

two. i don't really understand the world

three. i find it hard to tell people how i truly
feel

four. i seek validation from everyone

five. i crave a genuine friendship

six. no matter who i'm with, i've always felt
alone

seven. i wish i knew how to truly love myself

eight. i am so nervous for the future

loving you is the most important thing i will

ever do, because you are the only one i want,

the only one who cares and who wants me.

i want you too feel inspired by my beauty,

my intelligence,

not threatened

hope

can't you tell,

the world is transforming

into a calmer place

i've learnt i have to believe

i will be okay,

otherwise i have nothing

i'm too in love

with how my life is now

for me to waste it

on a man,

i can make myself happy

i think today

i properly saw the true me for the first time

in many years,

i wiped the steam from my mirror

and looked into my own eye

and saw the spark that used to be in them,

that shine

of hope and fight,

the girl i saw took my breath away,

she was beautiful,

radiant,

intelligent,

i touched my face

and couldn't believe

the wonders i was seeing,

the person i had transformed into,

164

i spent years inside my old body

thinking i was destined

to live a life of misery,

today i realise i have finally

opened my eyes to the future

and have transformed,

thank you,

thank you for helping me to live

i whisper to my reflection,

i love you

i need to keep telling myself

i can

i will

it's not impossible,

like a mantra

every time i open my eyes to meet the

morning sun,

otherwise i'm afraid

i'll meet a day where it all seems too hard

and i'll give up,

i need to believe

that life will have colour again

i think i'm starting

to love myself again

i want to applaud every single person

who survives,

and lives

when they have a dark shadow pulling them

back

from the inside

my heart has lived

amongst many days

of pain

and heartache,

so why would this one

be the end

my mind and body

are finally wanting

the same things

one day it'll hurt less,

you'll hear that song and it won't make you
cry,

you'll put on that jacket and you won't be
reminded of their scent,

you'll go to sleep and won't have nightmares
about what they did to you,

yet you'll dream about the future,

yes, it may take time,

and the healing might hurt,

but at least you'll be free

stop trying to find a new home

somewhere else,

the place you're already in

is quite magical itself

this won't last forever

keep telling yourself that

and one day you'll believe it

-hope

work at your own pace

and you'll be successful enough

your pain will lead you to your happiness

let yourself be free

i wake up every day

a better version of myself

listen to the people

with a smaller voice than you

yes you are beautiful,

it's undeniable,

but you are also

smart

brave

sacred

powerful

kind

and so much more,

don't determine your worth

on your looks

you're not just you. you are a heart. a mind. a soul. the people you love. the people who love you. a community. a warm body surrounding a city of blood and power. you are so much more that you think you are.

the more pain that i feel

the more words i write

my hands spiral out of control

as the words spill from my healing heart,

i write in hope

that my words may heal others

the way they healed me

you are finally free,

let yourself heal

Printed in Great Britain
by Amazon